# The U.S. Capitol

## Introducing Primary Sources

by Kathryn Clay

CAPSTONE PRESS
a capstone imprint

Little Explorer is published by Capstone Press,
1710 Roe Crest Drive, North Mankato, Minnesota 56003
www.mycapstone.com

**Library of Congress Cataloging-in-Publication Data**
Library of Congress Cataloging-in-Publication Data is available on the Library of Congress website.
ISBN 978-1-5157-6354-3 (library binding)
ISBN 978-1-5157-6359-8 (paperback)
ISBN 978-1-5157-6363-5 (eBook PDF)

**Editorial Credits**
Brenda Haugen, editor; Veronica Scott, designer; Kelli Lageson, media researcher;
Tori Abraham, production specialist

Our very special thanks to Jim Barber, Historian, National Portrait Gallery, Smithsonian, for his
curatorial review. Capstone would also like to thank the following at Smithsonian Enterprises: Kealy
Gordon, Product Development Manager, Ellen Nanney, Licensing Manager, Brigid Ferraro, Vice
President, Education and Consumer Products, Carol LeBlanc, Senior Vice President, Education and
Consumer Products, and Christopher A. Liedel, President.

**Photo Credits**
We would like to thank the following for permission to reproduce photographs: Alamy: Kumar
Sriskandan, 27; Architect of the Capitol: 8, 9 (top), 16, 17, 24, 25; Capstone Press, 5; Getty Images:
National Geographic Magazines/Scott S. Warren, 2, UIG/Encyclopaedia Brittanica, 7; Granger, NYC
- All rights reserved, 19; Library of Congress: 9 (bottom), 10, 11, 12 (left and right), 13, 14, 15, 18, 20
(right), 28; Shutterstock: Alberto Zamorano, 4, Black Russian Studio, cover, Joseph Sohm, 20 (left), Pete
Hoffman, 21, PhotosbyAndy, 23, Sean Pavone, 6, ValeStock, 26, William Ju, 29

Printed in the United States of America.
010399F17

# Table of Contents

# Primary Sources

People often write about major events in letters or diaries. These items are called primary sources. They are created at the time of an event. They help to paint a picture of important historical events. Other items such as photos, statues, and newspaper articles are also primary sources. Building designs and maps tell the history of the U.S. Capitol building.

The U.S. Capitol building is in Washington, D.C.

The U.S. Capitol is a sign of democracy. In a democracy, people vote for their leaders.

## The U.S. Capitol at a Glance

- located in Washington, D.C.
- slightly larger than four football fields
- has 540 rooms, 658 windows, and 850 doorways
- has its own post office
- U.S. Capitol is on the back of the $50 bill (below)

The U.S. Capitol is where members of Congress meet. Congress is made up of the Senate and the House of Representatives. These leaders vote on new laws.

# The Residence Act

Until 1790 the United States did not have a permanent capital city. Lawmakers met in Philadelphia, Pennsylvania. The president lived in Philadelphia.

The Declaration of Independence and U.S. Constitution were signed in Independence Hall in Philadelphia.

Congress passed the Residence Act on July 16. This meant an area of land near the Potomac River would become the nation's capital city. The city was later named Washington, D.C.

In 1791 Thomas Jefferson sketched a plan for the development of Washington, D.C.

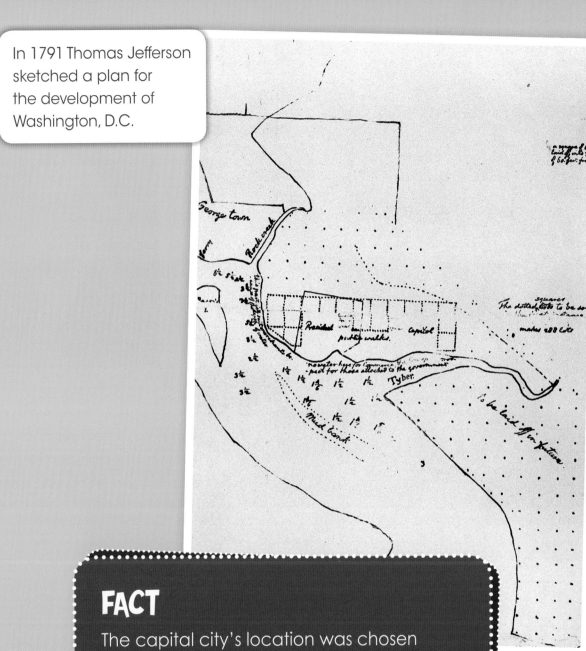

# FACT

The capital city's location was chosen because it lay between the northern and southern states.

# Choosing a Design

In 1792 a competition was held to find a design for the Capitol building. The prize was $500. Seventeen people sent designs. None of them were chosen. Three months later William Thornton, a doctor from the British West Indies, submitted a plan. His design looked like a Roman temple. It had many pillars and a large dome on top. President George Washington liked the design. Thornton won the prize.

a 1930 painting of Dr. William Thornton by George B. Matthews

## The Original Architect

French architect Pierre Charles L'Enfant was supposed to design the Capitol and oversee its construction. But he fought with builders. L'Enfant was fired when he refused to share his design plans. He said they were all in his head.

Dr. Thornton's designs for the U.S. Capitol

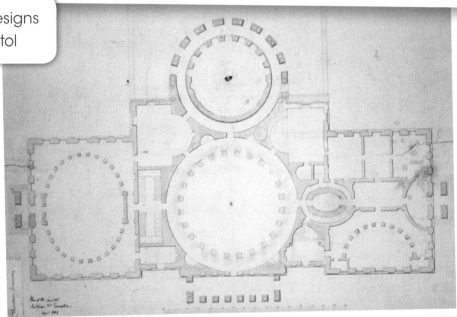

## FACT

Architect James Hoban was in charge of the Capitol's construction. Hoban also designed the White House.

# Building Begins

George Washington laid the cornerstone of the U.S. Capitol on September 18, 1793. Sandstone was brought in from Virginia on boats. It was hard to find builders to work on the Capitol. At the time, Washington, D.C., was not yet a major city. Few people wanted to work on the building in the wilderness.

a 1920 painting by Clyde De Land of George Washington laying the cornerstone at the U.S. Capitol

Builders weren't given enough money to complete the entire Capitol building. Instead they focused on the north wing.

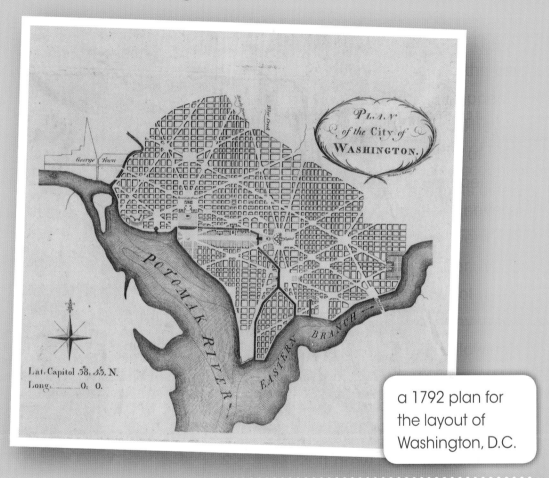

PLAN of the City of WASHINGTON.

a 1792 plan for the layout of Washington, D.C.

## FACT
Builders used marble rather than sandstone during later construction because marble lasts longer.

# North Wing

The Senate first met in the north wing of the Capitol on November 17, 1800. Though most of the north wing was completed, parts of the third floor were still unfinished. This area was to be used by the public to view Senate meetings. The area was finally completed in 1805.

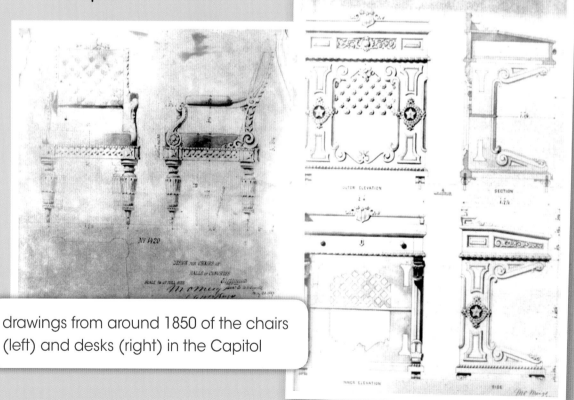

drawings from around 1850 of the chairs (left) and desks (right) in the Capitol

Because the north wing was the only completed part of the U.S. Capitol, the Supreme Court and the Library of Congress were also first housed here. The Library of Congress remained in the north wing until 1805. The Supreme Court met in the north wing from 1810 to 1860. It now meets nearby in its own building.

The Supreme Court Building was completed in 1935.

**FACT**

The Senate is made up of 100 senators. Citizens vote for their senators. Each state elects two senators every six years.

# South Wing

With the north wing complete, builders began work on the south wing. The south wing is where the House of Representatives meets.

an 1803 drawing of the plan for the south wing

The Car of History clock appears in the center of this 1803 drawing of what was once the main entrance to the House chamber.

The House first met at the Capitol in 1807, even though parts of the south wing were still unfinished. With money running low, the wing wasn't completed until 1811. A wooden walkway connected the north and south wings.

## The House of Representatives

The House of Representatives is made up of 435 people. The number of representatives a state has is based on each state's population. California has 53 representatives. Seven states with the smallest populations, including North Dakota, Vermont, and Alaska, each only have one representative. Elections for representatives are held every two years.

# Capitol Fire

During the War of 1812 (1812–1814), British soldiers set fire to buildings throughout Washington, D.C. The soldiers piled up furniture inside the U.S. Capitol's chambers and lit it on fire. The congressional chambers, Library of Congress, and Supreme Court were all badly damaged.

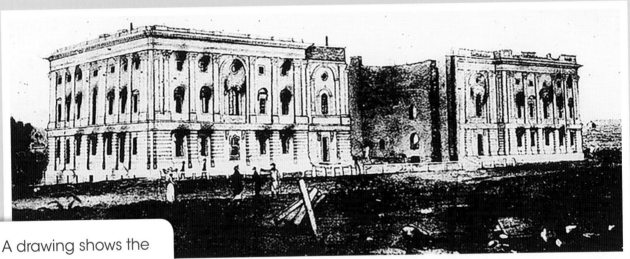

A drawing shows the damage to the U.S. Capitol after the fire on August 24, 1814.

## FACT

British soldiers also set fire to the White House. The White House was rebuilt in 1817.

Workers scrubbed the blackened walls. They spent four years rebuilding the U.S. Capitol. A temporary meeting place for Congress was built across the street. This building was called the Old Brick Capitol. It was later used as a prison during the Civil War (1861–1865).

A 1970s painting inside the Capitol shows the fire that damaged the bulding.

## The War of 1812

The War of 1812 was fought between the United States and Great Britain. Britain also was at war with France and tried to keep the United States from trading with the French. The British captured U.S. ships. American soldiers fought back. Both countries signed a peace treaty on December 24, 1814.

# Capitol Under Construction

By 1850 the Capitol was no longer large enough to hold all the members of Congress. The country had added new states. The U.S. population grew and so did the number of lawmakers. New construction doubled the size of the building.

An 1860 photo shows the Capitol under construction.

Construction continued during the Civil War. At the start of the war, the Capitol was used as a hospital and bakery. It also housed Union troops. The soldiers occupied the Rotunda and both chambers. They held loud, fake Congressional sessions to pass the time.

A wood engraving from a newspaper shows the Eighth Massachusetts Regiment living in the roofless Rotunda in 1861.

**FACT**

The soldiers' barracks smelled so bad, the architect refused to have his office in the Capitol.

# Dome and Rotunda

The Capitol's dome did not always look like it does today. The first dome was covered in copper. But with the additions in the 1850s, the old dome looked too small. A much larger cast-iron dome was added in 1866. The cost for the dome was $1 million.

In 1993 the *Statue of Freedom* was removed for restoration.

The *Statue of Freedom* atop the Capitol is made of bronze.

The *Statue of Freedom* rests on top of the dome. This statue stands 19.5 feet (6 meters) tall and weighs 15,000 pounds (6,800 kilograms).

The Rotunda is a round room in the center of the building below the large dome. Its walls are decorated with paintings and sculptures.

## FACT

It took the artist 11 months to paint *Aptheosis of Washington* in the eye of the Rotunda. The people in the painting are 15 feet tall!

Constantino Brumidi painted the *Aptheosis of Washington* in 1865.

# Capitol Crypt

A large, round room on the Capitol's first floor is called the Crypt. The room includes 40 sandstone columns that hold up the Rotunda on the second floor.

No one is buried in the Capitol Crypt.

Builders planned for George Washington and his wife, Martha, to be buried in the Crypt. A statue of the president was to be placed in the center. But Washington did not want to be buried at the Capitol. He was buried at his home in Mount Vernon, Virginia.

Mount Vernon, which was George Washington's home, overlooks the Potomac River, which also flows past Washington, D.C.

# National Statuary Hall

The National Statuary Hall is also known as the Old Hall of the House. It is near the Rotunda. States can donate up to two statues to be displayed. Currently the room holds 35 statues. The others are placed throughout the building.

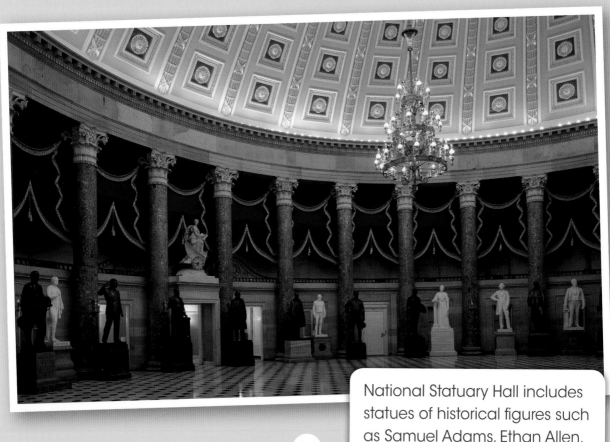

National Statuary Hall includes statues of historical figures such as Samuel Adams, Ethan Allen, and Helen Keller.

The House of Representatives met in the National Statuary Hall from 1819 to 1857. But the tall, curved ceilings created echoes. Representatives struggled to hear one another.

**FACT**

The largest statue was donated by Hawaii. The bronze statue of Hawaiian King Kamehameha I (1758–1819) weighs about 15,000 pounds (6,800 kg).

KAMEHAMEHA I

FIRST KING
OF

# The U.S. Capitol Today

Through the years, the Capitol building has had many updates. More than $100 million has been spent on construction and maintenance. Indoor plumbing, electricity, and high-speed Internet have been added.

Work to repair cracks and other damage to the dome began in 2013 and was completed in 2016.

The official Capitol Visitor Center opened in 2008. Today the U.S. Capitol is a popular place for tourists. About 3 million to 5 million people visit the U.S. Capitol each year to see democracy in action.

A guide leads a group on a tour of the Capitol Rotunda.

# Timeline

1790    Residence Act is passed

1790    contest is held to find a design

1793    construction begins

1800    the Senate meets in the Capitol building for the first time

1807    House of Representatives meets in the Capitol for the first time

1811    south wing is complete

Adelaide Johnson sculpted the images of suffragists Susan B. Anthony, Lucretia Mott, and Elizabeth Cady Stanton that are found in the Capitol.

**August 24, 1814**   British soldiers set fire to the Capitol

**1850**   Capitol under construction

**1861–1863**   cast-iron dome is built

**1898**   fireproofing is completed throughout the Capitol after a fire damages part of the building

**1958–1962**   90 additional rooms are added to the east-central front area of the building

**2008**   Capitol Visitor Center opens

# Glossary

**architect**—a person who designs and draws plans for buildings, bridges, and other construction projects

**capital**—the city where a country's government meets and makes laws

**chamber**—a large room

**Congress**—the branch of the U.S. government that makes laws

**cornerstone**—the first brick or stone of a building that is going to be built

**crypt**—an underground room used as a burial site

**democracy**—a system of government where citizens vote for their leaders and lawmakers

**design**—a plan for how to build something

**dome**—a roof shaped like a cereal bowl

**permanent**—intended to last or remain unchanged

**pillar**—a tall structure made of stone, wood, or metal used to support a building or as decoration

**primary source**—an original document

**rotunda**—a round building or room

**Supreme Court**—the highest and most powerful court in the United States

**tourist**—a person who is visiting a place for fun

**treaty**—a formal agreement between countries

# Read More

Carr, Aaron. *Capitol Building*. American Icons. New York: Weigl, 2016.

Ferguson, Melissa. *American Symbols: What You Need to Know*. Fact Files. North Mankato, Minn: Capstone Press, 2017.

Lee, Georgia. *Tour the U.S. Capitol*. Infomax Common Core Readers. New York: Rosen, 2013.

Lee, Susan Schrader. *Secrets of Our Nation's Capital: Weird and Wonderful Facts About Washington, D.C.* New York: Sterling Children's Books, 2016.

# Internet Sites

Use FactHound to find Internet sites related to this book.

Visit www.facthound.com

Just type in 9781515763543 and go.

Super-cool stuff!

Check out projects, games and lots more at
**www.capstonekids.com**

# Critical Thinking Questions

1. Few builders wanted to work on the Capitol because it was in the wilderness. What challenges would the builders have faced?

2. How was the U.S. Capitol used during the Civil War?

3. Why do you think British soldiers set fire to buildings in Washington. D.C., during the War of 1812?

# Index